The Thoughts Of ME!
/ मेरे मन की बाते !

A collection of my poems

Akshita Garg

BookLeaf
Publishing
India | USA | UK

Made with ❤ on the BookLeaf Publishing Platform
www.bookleafpub.in
www.bookleafpub.com

Dedication

I want to dedicate this book to my parents, my younger sibling, and my god, Lord Krishna.

Preface

I began writing poems during lockdown and found a way to express my thoughts, which helped me overcome those tough times and find solace. The poems written in this book are a collection of writings in two languages spoken by the author, i.e, Hindi and English. I want anyone who finds my work interesting to read my poems with an open heart. All the best!

Acknowledgements

Dear gentle readers,
I would like to express my sincere gratitude to my family, friends, and everyone who supported me throughout this creative journey. Your love, encouragement, and belief in me have made this book possible.
A special thanks to the editors and publishers for their valuable guidance, and to my readers, whose connection to my work is the greatest reward.
Finally, I acknowledge the world around me—its beauty and struggles—that continually inspires my poetry.
With heartfelt thanks,

Akshita Garg

1. Happiness

What is happiness?
Is it a reality or an illusion,
does it really depend on your vision?

✿

If love is happiness
then it is like a sweet poison,
the poison that can kill you,
but you still want it.

✿

If caring is happiness,
then it is the suicide by a soul,
"who are you gonna care for in this cruel world",
but you still do it.

✿

If truth is happiness,
then it brings chaos for some,
and peace to some,
but it will come out.

✿

If lie is happiness,
then make sure your lie
settles someone's life.

✿

If memories are happiness,

we wanna stay in them
because no matter what,
this life moves with happiness.
✿✿

2. Love at first sight!

At 5, saw her on her pony,
she was focused on back ride,
I noticed she lived on countryside.

As she was about to leave,
our eyes met,
She was an angel, in the breeze and in that sunset.

That night, I couldn't sleep.
was I in love, had a feeling of what kind,
But the idea of her stayed in my mind.

As I grew, watched her grow,
wanted to talk to her,
but had no clue, what to do.

One day she left,
with no whereabouts,
My heart broke in silence,
It was a war without violence.

This made me think,
i can either move on or,
become an obsessive lover.

I decided to leave it behind,
and finally live without boundaries of love.

3. A 'Bad' queen

On a lone island,
lived a Queen,
Surrounded by the ocean,
ocean of grief.
She grew up living inside the palace,
as innocent she was,
saw the world from a window in the fort,
where the sun would shine the brightest,
the birds could sing for the lord.
One day, she was left behind to rule,
All alone and young,
She turned to a friend,
who turned her cruel.
Her cruelty became a reason
for the loss of every single breath,
later on she was only one on the holm.
That was the rise of
"The Bad Queen".
And after that no bird sang,
never did the sun shine.

4. Self

Every moment in my life, I believed in self-cursing.
My mind was like a landfill of thoughts,
where soul came crushing.

Mirror Mirror on the wall did not make sense,
I became a person who would only approve of a Man, of substance.

Worries about my life choices came daunting, "where will I find that peace I wanted??"
Suddenly, I heard an inner voice,
Who told me " my child you need not fright",
"your god will accept you one day, and every thing will be alright".

5. Love, lies

How do you feel
when no one gives you importance,
when you have tried everything, but it was not working
the way you wanted?

✿

My heart broke several times in the process to mend his,
It felt like my universe was going down,
But his heart was never mine,
seeing him happy was just fine.

✿

Now that I think about it,
Only thing that comes to my mind is,
Did I do something wrong? Was I not good enough for
him?

✿

I still don't know whether I deserved his love,
But I know that love never deserved me.

6. Flower

A little flower, set on it's soil,
minding it's own business,
guarding it's own soul.

✿

Flourishing under it's gardner,
it was left to look after by another grower,
devil in disguise.

✿

The flower, unknown of the intention
of the grower,
smiled at him, but did not understand the smile
of the foul plucker.

✿

The innocence of the flower was gone,
it was dead (inside her)
her love was, forever , gone.

7. बचपन की बात है।

बचपन की बात है,
हर साल नानी के घर जाया करते थे।
जब न कोई बोझ था, न कोई परेशानी,

जो था वो बस हँसी और खुशियों की रवानी।
अब कहाँ जाते हैं उस रास्ते,

न उठते हैं कदम
क्योंकि न रहा वो समय,
और न रहा वो बचपन।
बचपन की बात है...

8. यादें

ज़िंदगी के कुछ पल मुझे हमेशा याद आएँगे

पता नहीं क्यों ये वक़्त भागता चला जाता है,
आज कब कल बन जाता है।

कभी मुस्कान दे जाता है, कभी खामोशी,
कुछ लम्हे छोड़ जाते हैं गहरी सी कोई कमी।

भविष्य में भी ये पल सताएंगे,
कुछ बीते लम्हे मुझे बहुत याद आएंगे।

वो बचपन की बातें, वो नानी का आँगन,
वो बेफ़िक्री के दिन, और ख़्वाबों का सावन।

अब तो हर चेहरा थोड़ा अनजान सा लगता है,
वो अपनापन भी जैसे कहीं खो गया है।

पर दिल के किसी कोने में वो दिन अब भी मुस्कुराते हैं,
जब भी थक जाता हूँ, वो यादें मुझे फिर से जीना सिखाते हैं।

9. वो सुकून भरे दिन

एक ज़माना था जब ज़िंदगी आसान थी,
आसमान नीला और शाम बहुत शांत थी।

न कोई कष्ट था, न कोई शोर,
गया वो दौर... कितना था वो कोमल और गौर।

काश कहीं लौट के आ जाए,
बस कहीं लौट के आ जाए।

वो चाय की चुस्की, वो आँगन की बात,
बिना वजह की हँसी, वो दिल से की सौगात।

अब तो सब कुछ है, पर वो सुकून नहीं,
हर चेहरे पर हँसी है, पर वो जुनून नहीं।

कभी-कभी सोचता हूँ... क्या वक़्त थम सकता है?
क्या बीते हुए पल फिर से रम सकता है?

10. मन का द्वंद्व

एक संकोच है मेरे मन में,
क्या ही होगी गलती उस मासूम की?
वो तो बस माँ-बाप के साथ घूमने गया था।

तुम कहते हो मज़हब नहीं सिखाता आपस में बैर रखना,
पर हमला तो मज़हब के नाम पर हुआ था।

तुम कहते हो वो नफरत फैला रहे हैं,
उनका क्या, जो पहले से ही द्वेष लेकर बैठे हैं दिल में?
एक संकोच है मेरे मन में,
क्या शब्दों से बुझा पाऊँगा ये अग्नि?
क्या मैं समझा सकता हूँ उस चीत्कार को,
जो मेरे भीतर गूंजती है, पर बाहर नहीं आ पाती?

या क्या वो मासूम,
जिसकी आँखों में डर और कशमकश है,
कभी मेरे शब्दों का मुहावरा बन पाएगा?
एक संकोच है मेरे मन में।

11. एक नियम

ज़िंदगी का एक नियम होता है

ज़िंदगी का एक नियम होता है,
कि वो बिन रुके चलती रहनी चाहिए।

आने वाला आएगा और जाने वाला जाएगा,
दुःख उसका नहीं जो चला जाता है,
उसका है जो पीछे छूट जाता है,
पल दो पल में जीवन बदल जाता है।

ज़िंदगी का एक नियम होता है,
कि वो बिन रुके चलती रहनी चाहिए।

12. ना आए उसके कृष्ण

बचपन से कहानियों में सुनती थी,
दोस्ती और प्यार की दास्तानें पढ़ा करती थी।

सोचती थी, शायद यही उसकी भी कहानी होगी,
कोई राजकुमार आएगा और ले जाएगा उसे अपने संग।

समय बीता, वक्त बीता, बीते कई वर्ष,
लेकिन नहीं आया राजकुमार, न वो दोस्त, न वो प्यार।

जैसे राधा-कृष्ण की लीला की आस में,
वो राधा ढूढती रही अपने कृष्ण को।

पर वो पगली क्या जानती थी किस्मत के इस तर्क को,
ना राजकुमार आया, ना आए उसके कृष्ण,
वो प्रेम उसकी तरफ़ नहीं आया,
वो प्यार उसकी तरफ़ नहीं आया।

13. अंतर

तुमने कहा – जाने दो,
तुमने कहा – प्रतिक्रिया मत दो,
तुमने कहा – कोई नफरत करे तो भी ठीक है।

मैंने जाने दिया, मैंने कुछ नहीं कहा,
स्वीकार कर लिया कि हर कोई तुम्हें प्यार नहीं करेगा।

तुमने मुझे वो बना दिया जो मैं कभी नहीं थी,
तुमने मुझे भीतर से बदल दिया,
जबकि तुम तो सिर्फ एक याद बनकर ही मौजूद थे।

कुछ तो था तुममें, जो सबसे अलग था,
क्योंकि जब ये दुनिया मुझ पर कीचड़ उछालती थी,
तुम अपने शब्दों से, अपनी सोच से,
मुझे एक सुकून दे जाते थे।

14. संघर्ष

ज़िंदगी में हारने पर याद रखना ए मुसाफ़िर,
कि क़िस्मत कभी भी आज़माती है।

पर इंसान तभी हारता है,
जब वो खुद हार मान ले।

वरना क़िस्मत कितनी भी आज़मा ले,
हरजाना तो किस्मत को भी भरना पड़ता है।

वक़्त ऐसा खेल खेलता है,
कि राजा और रंक में फर्क समझ नहीं आता।

इसलिए चलते रहो मुसाफ़िर,
मुश्किलें चाहे जितनी भी हों।
हर अंधेरी रात के बाद
एक नयी सुबह जरूर होती है।

ना थको, ना रुको,
बस यकीन रखो खुद पर,
क्योंकि मंज़िल उन्हीं को मिलती है
जो हौसले से चलते हैं,
हर मोड़ पर, हर हाल में

15. Set me free

Enough of the judgments, no more atonements,
I'm done paying debts for your disappointments.
No longer your mirror, no longer your mold,
I won't shrink myself to fit stories you told.

I want to grow – like the trees, untamed,
With roots that dig deep and a soul unchained.
Let the sky stretch wide and the winds run wild,
I'll dance with the storms like a fearless child.

You placed your labels, built invisible walls,
Assumed my worth by how softly I fall.
But I'm not your silence, not your shame,
I'm rising now; I'll reclaim my name.

There's a fire inside that refuses to die,
Not born to crawl, I was made to fly.
So don't clip these wings with your "should" and "must,"
I'm done placing my dreams in your rust.

I want to breathe where the wild things sing,
Not in chains but on wide-open wings.
No more pretending, no need to agree –

I am who I am.
Just set me free.

16. वीरगति

जान जोखिम में डालकर,
वो चला राही प्यार का,
हाथों में बारूद और दिल में जज़्बा,
चाँदनी रात थी,
उसके चेहरे पर मुस्कान थी,
चला गया वो वीर बहादुर,
जिसकी क़िस्मत देश पर क़ुर्बान थी।

यही है फ़र्क उसमे और मुझमें,
मेरे हिस्से में कहाँ देश के लिए बलिदान देना लिखा है।

17. Talk in Silence!

We spoke no words, yet shared a storm,
In quiet stares, our hearts grew warm.
Your silence wrapped around my soul,
In silent deep, a story told.

In stillness, you heard my cries,
In silence, I saw your skies.
No echo, yet the message was clear
You were far, but always near.

Your silence wasn't empty space,
It held a touch, in soft embrace.
We didn't need the world to see,
In silence, it belonged to me.

No need to say what eyes confess,
In silent love, we feel the rest.
The loudest words, the deepest touch,
Are often those that speak not much.

Between your sigh and my still breath,
We danced on edges, life and death.
Not every voice needs to be heard
Some hearts are louder than a word.

Between your sigh and my still breath,
We danced on edges, life and death.
Not every voice needs to be heard
Some hearts are louder than a word.

18. The Girl Who Believed

Born with high spirits,
With a goal to stand apart,
Pushing her limits,
To leave behind a mark.

She dreamt of a life,
Where she would truly thrive,
Little did she know,
Life's less of a flower
And more like a knife.

Now, at the age called "grown,"
She looks back,
Wondering,
Was it all worth it?

And somewhere deep inside,
The young girl in her replied
IT WAS.

19. मासूमियत

एक वक़्त था, जब आँखों में ख्वाब सजे थे,
दिल में न सवाल थे, न कोई धोखे पले थे।

बेमतलब की बातें, सच्ची मुस्कान,
हर चीज़ में ढूढ लेते थे हम भगवान।

न पैसे की फिक्र, न नाम की चाह,
बस मिट्टी से खेलना ही था हर राहत की राह।

अब बड़े हो गए हैं, पर खो दी वो चीज़,
जिसे कहते हैं मासूमियत – जो थी सबसे अज़ीज़।

काश लौट आए वो दिन फिर से,
जहाँ हर रिश्ता था दिल से, बिना किसी डर के।